Dealing
with
Doubt

The Journey Study Series

Searching for Hope

Living as a Christian

Leaving a Legacy

Dealing with Doubt

Confronting the Enemies Within

Embracing the Good News

Building a Christ-Centered Home

Learning to Pray

The Facilitator's Guide

Dealing with Doubt

A Thomas Nelson Study Series
Based on *The Journey*
by
BILLY GRAHAM

THOMAS NELSON
Since 1798

NASHVILLE   DALLAS   MEXICO CITY   RIO DE JANEIRO   BEIJING

Published in Nashville, Tennessee. Thomas Nelson is a trademark of Thomas Nelson, Inc.

Thomas Nelson, Inc., titles may be purchased in bulk for educational, business, fund-raising, or sales promotional use. For information, please e-mail SpecialMarkets@ThomasNelson.com.

Unless otherwise noted, all Scripture quotations are taken from *The Holy Bible*, NEW INTERNATIONAL VERSION®. NIV®. Copyright © 1973, 1978, 1984 by International Bible Society. Used by permission of Zondervan. All rights reserved.

Dealing with Doubt: A Thomas Nelson Study Series Based on The Journey *by Billy Graham*

ISBN-13: 978-1-4185-1771-7
ISBN-10: 1-4185-1771-2

Printed in the United States of America

07 08 09 10 11 RRD 5 4 3 2 1

Contents

1. Can We Be Sure? / 1

2. Our Firm Foundation / 19

3. The Unending Battle / 39

4. Our Constant Helper / 61

5. Strength for Each Day / 83

6. Suffering and Loss / 105

Notes / 125

1

Can
We Be
Sure?

T O GET THE MOST FROM THIS STUDY GUIDE, READ
pages 63–67 of *The Journey*.

*Is uncertainty the only certainty in life? Uncertainty
and insecurity seem to be the watchwords of our generation. Any certainty in this uncertain world, many
have concluded, is little more than wishful thinking.
Must uncertainty also be true of our spiritual lives?*

BILLY GRAHAM
The Journey

THINK ABOUT IT

God never made a promise that was too good to be true.

—DWIGHT L. MOODY[1]

*I know whom I have believed, and am convinced that he
is able to guard what I have entrusted to him for that day.*

—2 TIMOTHY 1:12

So many things in life are uncertain that it's difficult for many people to accept God's message without having doubts. People who experience God's love still may convince themselves that God couldn't possibly love them. Doubts can overwhelm new or shallow-rooted faith and leave people wondering if they really have a relationship with God.

Doubts are a normal part of life. We doubt things on earth, so it's easy to doubt the things of God. Yet God's promises are His promises. What He has said in the past remains true today. God never changes and never goes back on His Word. If He did, then He wouldn't be God.

We run into trouble when we try to give God human characteristics because God is so much more. But that's all we understand. When we are let down by a person, we can easily believe God will let us down. It's true that God often doesn't come through in the way and timing you expected, but that's not a flaw in God; it's a flaw in your expectations. Let's take a closer look at doubt and how we can overcome it in our spiritual lives.

REWIND

What are some things you expected God to do but He didn't do?

_____

_____

_____

_____

How was your faith affected by these events?

_____

_____

_____

When reevaluating the situations mentioned above, what mistakes did you make?

_____ I looked at things from my perspective rather than from God's perspective.

_____ I gave God a "to do" list rather than seeking His direction.

_____ I misunderstood what it means to trust God.

_____ I had an inadequate understanding of God's Word.

_____ Other: _____

In this life, uncertainty is certain! Take a look at today's headlines and you won't find many things that encourage you. Get to know your neighbors and you'll discover they, too, have doubts about the state of our world. The family is disintegrating, and biblical values are being challenged. The coming generations are skeptical about their employers, the economy, world peace, and just about everything else. Some of this skepticism is justified. Ours is no longer a society of trust. Today, people spend countless hours developing scams that are intended to take advantage of trusting people.

But does cultural uncertainty automatically lead to spiritual uncertainty? Is it possible to really trust God to keep His promises? What causes people to doubt their faith?

JOURNEY THROUGH GOD'S WORD

We use the term *backsliding* in a variety of situations, yet there is some question about the biblical accuracy of the term. In the Old Testament, *backsliding* is used in reference to Israel's inconsistent relationship with God.

Because of Israel's lack of faith in Him, God declared that the nation was backsliding (Isaiah 57:17). In Jeremiah 3, God uses *backsliding* as an adjective describing the manner in which Israel had behaved in their relationship with Him.

In Hosea 11:7, God pointed out that His people called to Him but were inconsistent in their relationships with Him.[2]

Backsliding in the Old Testament involved not only turning away from God but serving other gods. The Israelites were strongly influenced by the Canaanite religions that were practiced by the people who inhabited the Promised Land. The Israelites were disobedient to God's instruction to wipe out the pagan people and destroy their religion. As a result, the sensual nature of pagan religion appealed to many Israelites, so they polluted their faith with pagan practices and, over time, turned away from the pure practice of authentic faith in God.

Our culture is in a similar situation. Because the demands of real faith are difficult, we attempt to soften it with feel-good sermons and "we're all OK" Bible studies. We avoid the hard truths of Scripture because we aren't willing to let it transform our lives. We want God to meet our needs, but we don't want Him to get involved in changing our lives.

Though we aren't the Israelites trying to live in the Promised Land, we still are spiritually distracted and subject to backsliding. It's an old term with a modern reality.

Doubts certainly are real, and they seem to pop up at the most inconvenient times. A closer investigation into the causes of doubt might help us develop a strategy for defending ourselves against Satan's attacks.

RETHINK

What are some things that have caused you to question your faith or your salvation?

_____

_____

_____

_____

_____

How can you know for sure that God really loves and cares for you? How can you overcome the natural doubts that come as a result of living in a sinful world? You must first consider one truth about Satan—if he can't keep you from Christ, he will try to make you doubt your salvation.

What happens to your spiritual effectiveness when you begin doubting your salvation?

_____

_____

_____

_____

Doubting your salvation is spiritually debilitating. It puts you in a position where you cannot accomplish those things God has prescribed for you to do. You won't talk to the people you should talk to; you won't encourage the people you should encourage. Satan has a way of distracting you at precisely the point at which you should be doing something for God. One of his most effective distraction techniques is doubt.

REFLECT

What causes Christians to doubt their salvation? After all that God has done, why would we question Him? Why do we question ourselves?

1. **We doubt our salvation because we still sin and fear God will reject us because of it.**

   We all have had moments when we felt as if we disappointed God, and rightfully so. However, when we disappoint God, He doesn't respond the same way as we do when someone disappoints us. We set ourselves up for doubt because we wrongly assume that salvation will result in a perfect life for us and for those we know who are saved. God never promised we would be perfect this side of heaven.

How do you respond to someone who disappoints you?

_____

_____

_____

Read Psalm 145:8. How does God respond when we disappoint Him?

_____

_____

_____

God doesn't expect us to be perfect; there has only been one perfect human—Jesus Christ. God does expect us to have an awareness of His desires for us and His will for our lives. He expects us to use His Word to learn right from wrong. He expects us to recognize sin in our lives and seek forgiveness when we fail Him. But nowhere in the Bible do we see God dissolve His relationship with anyone who truly trusts Him and gives his or her life to Him.

What happens when we expect other Christians to be perfect?

_____

_____

_____

_____

2. **We doubt our salvation because we depend solely on our emotions.**

   For many people, the conversion experience is emotional. Yet, after a while, the emotion fades. Without the emotion that accompanied their salvation, people can believe that salvation didn't really happen.

What happens when your faith depends solely on your emotions?

_____

_____

_____

_____

_____

Read Ephesians 4:14. In this verse, Paul mentions the danger of being tossed about by circumstances. Emotions can do the same thing. We can have emotional peaks and valleys that accompany different stages of life. We must separate our salvation from our emotions because we cannot sustain emotional highs for long periods of time.

People who depend solely on their emotions for spiritual stability often will misinterpret problems as God's way of getting them for something they have done. This is a topic that will be covered in more detail in a later lesson.

Emotional Christianity can cause problems because people believe that their faith is limited to situations in which the emotion is present. Certainly there are times when our faith is emotional, but we make a mistake when we make faith emotion-dependent.

3. **We also doubt our salvation because of misguided humility.**

   Some people argue that it is presumptuous to say that they know they will go to heaven when they die. They believe stating it is prideful and pride is a sin.

   Pride is a sin, but we aren't saved based on the presence or absence of pride in our lives. God saves us based on His mercy and grace.

Read Ephesians 2:8–9. What are the requirements for salvation?

_____

_____

_____

Our confidence in our salvation isn't based on us; it is based on our understanding of God's promises and His character. If we have faith in ourselves, we will never have access to heaven. However, faith in Christ opens the door to heaven, and that door can never be closed. You can know that you will go to heaven when you die. Think back to that moment when you accepted Jesus Christ as your Lord and Savior. You realized some things about yourself and you realized some things about God.

When you were saved, what did you realize about God?

_____

_____

_____

What did you realize about yourself?

_____

_____

_____

When you were saved, you confessed your sin and asked Jesus Christ to move in and take over your life. He willingly accepted your invitation to come into your life. Think about these facts.

1. If Jesus voluntarily left, His Word would be untrue.

2. If you invited Jesus to leave and He did, that would make you more powerful than Him.

3. If salvation wasn't permanent, why did God say, "Never will I leave you; never will I forsake you" (Hebrews 13:5)?

If we believe God will leave us, then we believe His Word to be untrue. If His Word is untrue, then we cannot trust it in regard to any aspect of life. But we know that God's Word is true; He is who the Bible says He is. When the doubts come, we must rely on the strength of Scripture and its reliability.

REACT

Our reaction to this lesson is twofold. First, there must be a time at which you consciously asked Jesus Christ to become your Lord and Savior. You don't get salvation as a part of the will of one of your ancestors. You must enter into that personal relationship because you chose to do so.

Recount the time when you first asked Jesus Christ to be your Lord and Savior.

_____

_____

_____

Second, you must take God at His Word. What God has said remains true. God's Word isn't subject to review or reinterpretation. It isn't outdated or irrelevant. God's Word is powerful and true. If you know that you asked Jesus Christ to be your Savior, then doubting your salvation says that you doubt God's Word.

Think about the last time you doubted your salvation. What was going on in your life at the time? What might have been some situational causes of your doubt?

_____

_____

_____

_____

By spending time with God on a daily basis, you can strengthen your relationship so that you can fend off the doubts that are sure to come. However, checking in with God once a week or letting everything else get between you and God weakens your spiritual life and makes you more susceptible to doubts about your salvation. Doubt is an indication of your spiritual strength.

> *God doesn't save us because of who we are or how good we are, nor can we ever claim we are better than others—because we aren't. God has saved us solely by His mercy and grace, and we can't take any credit for our salvation—none at all. Our confidence must be in Christ and Christ alone.*
>
> BILLY GRAHAM
> *The Journey*

What are three truths you learned in this study, and how will you apply each truth to your daily life?

1. _____

_____

_____

_____

2. _____

_____

_____

_____

3. _____

_____

_____

_____

2

Our
Firm
Foundation

To GET THE MOST FROM THIS STUDY GUIDE, READ
pages 67–73 of *The Journey*.

> *Just as a careful builder first lays a solid foundation*
> *before constructing a building, so God's Word gives us a*
> *solid foundation for building our spiritual lives. Why is*
> *this important? Because if we aren't sure whether or*
> *not God loves us, our journey through life will be hes-*
> *itant, uncertain, insecure. But if we have confidence*
> *in God's love, then our journey will be joyful, assured,*
> *and filled with hope.*
>
> BILLY GRAHAM
> *The Journey*

THINK ABOUT IT

We are not human beings having a spiritual experience.
We are spiritual beings having a human experience.
— TEILHARD DE CHARDIN[1]

For no one can lay any foundation other than the one already laid, which is Jesus Christ.

—1 CORINTHIANS 3:11

The assurance of salvation is such an important thing that God laid out in His Word irrefutable evidence of His never-ending love for us. As is stated in the verse above, the key element of our salvation rests in what Jesus did in life, on the cross, and after His death. We must hold these facts as undeniable truths. We can't go through life wondering if Jesus really lived and expect our faith to increase.

The strength of a skyscraper is dependent on its foundation. Likewise, the strength of our faith is dependent on our spiritual foundation. If your spiritual strength is tied to a person other than Jesus Christ, your faith will be subject to problems and doubts.

REWIND

What are some nonnegotiable facts related to your faith?

_____

_____

_____

What makes these facts nonnegotiable?

_____

_____

_____

_____

If anything God has said isn't really true, upon what can you base your faith?

_____

_____

_____

_____

One of the tough things to comprehend about God is His inability to go back on His promises. Everything God has promised will come true. It's part of who God is. If He ever fails to deliver on one promise, then every promise can be held suspect.

JOURNEY THROUGH GOD'S WORD

What is a promise? In our culture, it is a declaration that one will or will not do something. In other words, it is a vow. Many promises, however, don't carry much weight. An athlete will promise a championship; a retailer might promise low prices. Promises are little more than wishful thinking.

So, when we begin to consider God's promises, it is easy to transpose the modern meaning and apply uncertainty to our thoughts about God. When God promises peace, we interpret it to mean that there will be peace if everything goes as planned.

That's not the idea behind the concept of a promise in the Bible. God's promise is His announcement of His plans for His people. These plans include salvation and blessing. It is this certainty that is behind every mention of God's promises in Scripture.

God's initial promise to His people was that He would be their God, they would be His people, and He would live among them. The promise was restated in a variety of ways throughout Scripture and fully realized in the person of His Son, Jesus Christ.

God's promises have some common characteristics:

1. Promises concern what is good and enriching.

2. Promises concern the entire human race, not a select few.

3. Promises have continual fulfillment from generation to generation.

4. Promises are unconditional.[2]

As you can see, there are considerable differences between what we mean when we say "promise" and what God means. We must live with the certainty that God's promises will indeed be fulfilled in our lifetimes and in generations to come.

We often base our hope on situations that are questionable and variable. As we consider our faith, we must remember that authentic faith is based on the uncompromising truth of God's Word and the promises He has made. Satan wants nothing more than to confuse and frustrate you. He wants you to give up on God's promises. In a world that focuses on self-gratification, people often look for God's promises to be exclusively theirs. They fail to realize that God's promises are universal and for all people. Without an awareness of and commitment to God's promises, our faith is built on the sand.

RETHINK

Describe a time when your faith in God was its strongest.

_____

_____

_____

When was your faith in God its weakest?

_____

_____

_____

Read Psalm 62:7. Is this statement really true of you? Explain your response.

_____

_____

_____

One of the amazing characteristics of seasoned Christians is their ability to weather life's storms while holding on to their faith in God. Parents suffer the loss of a child and confess that God is up to something; they just aren't sure what it is. Faithful employees lose their jobs and hold to God's promise to meet their needs. The true test of our faith comes when times get tough.

Think about your last crisis. As you dealt with the issues you faced, what role did your faith play?

_____ I depended on it.

_____ I gave it lip service.

_____ I parked it until the problem was solved.

_____ I don't have any faith.

_____ I tried to have faith, but I didn't always succeed.

Most of us can admit to times when our faith in God wasn't as strong as it could have been or should have been. Maybe that's because our faith isn't built on the solid foundation that God intended. Let's take some time to investigate the foundation of real faith.

REFLECT

God has given us assurance of His love and protection for this life and the life to come. These are assurances we can stake our lives on.

1. **The rock of God's promises.**
   Because some people have deceived us, we have a tough time believing that God will be true to His Word. Yet that is a fact about God.

Read Psalm 18:30. What does this verse say about everything God has ever said?

_____

_____

_____

_____

Read Malachi 3:6 and fill in the blank: "I the LORD do not

_____ ."

What does this mean to you as you consider how God has dealt with biblical people?

_____ God will deal with me differently than He dealt with them.

_____ God will deal with me the same as He dealt with them.

_____ I'm honestly not sure how God will deal with me.

God's promise of eternal security means that you and I do not have to go through life wondering if we get to keep our salvation.

Read Romans 8:38–39 and John 10:28. Which of the following is true, based on these verses?

_____ It is impossible to know if you are saved.

_____ Salvation is temporary.

_____ You cannot lose your salvation.

_____ Satan can take us away from God.

Our salvation was always in God's plans. Throughout the Old Testament, God promised that He would send a Messiah.

Prophets expressed God's plans to cultures who misunderstood what they meant. Yet the promises were true. Long before Jesus Christ was born, the prophet Isaiah spoke of His life (see Isaiah 53:5, 11). God promised and delivered; that's His character.

2. **The rock of Christ's finished work.**
   In John 19:30, we see Jesus' declaration that "it is finished." But what was finished? Jesus wasn't speaking about just His life and His ministry. He was making the declaration that the purpose for which He came to earth had been completed.

What was Jesus' purpose in coming to the world? Read Luke 19:10.

_____ **Jesus came to be a good teacher.**

_____ **Jesus came to save the lost.**

_____ **Jesus came to create a new religion.**

Jesus accomplished for us what we could not do for ourselves—He opened a way for us to get to heaven that is not based on anything we do for Him. If our salvation is based on our works, then we cannot be sure we are saved. If our salvation is based on our goodness, then we cannot be sure we are saved. However, because our salvation is based on what Jesus did, we know it is secure.

How do we know His death really won our salvation? We know it for one reason: because Jesus Christ rose from the dead. No event in human history is more startling or more significant. It proves beyond doubt that Jesus was indeed who He claimed to be: the unique Son of God, sent from heaven to save us from our sins. It also confirms that He has conquered for all time the forces of sin and death and hell and Satan. Christ's sacrifice is complete—and the proof is His resurrection from the dead.

BILLY GRAHAM
The Journey

Jesus' death by itself might not seem to be that significant—plenty of great people die. But how many come back to life? We honor historical figures with graves that serve as a memorial of their lives. Yet, Jesus isn't significant only because of His death; He is significant because of what happened after His death.

Read the following Scriptures and list below each one the fact related to Jesus' death.

Matthew 27:59–60

Matthew 27:66

_____

Matthew 28:2

_____

Matthew 28:9–10

_____

Jesus died, was buried, and the tomb was guarded. However, there was an earthquake and the tomb was opened. Jesus rose from the dead and spoke with His followers. Historians have recorded it; skeptics have doubted. The fact remains that Jesus lived, died, and was raised to life so that you and I could have the opportunity to spend eternity in heaven with God.

You can't do anything to make your salvation better or more secure. All you must do is accept Jesus' offer of eternal life and commit to being His disciple.

3. **The rock of the Spirit's witness.**
   Like we said earlier, salvation isn't dependent on emotions. You aren't more saved on the days you feel better and less saved on the days you feel worse. How you feel has nothing to do with your salvation.

Read Romans 8:16. According to this verse, what is the role of the Holy Spirit?

_____

_____

_____

_____

Read 2 Corinthians 1:22. According to this verse, what is the role of the Holy Spirit?

_____

_____

_____

_____

Salvation changes people. You can't come face to face with the God of the universe and walk away unaffected! When God comes to live in you, you begin to develop His attitudes, behaviors, desires, and priorities.

Think about your life. Where are you in the following areas? Place an X on the line.

The way I've always been   Just like God

a. Attitudes _____

b. Thoughts _____

c. Behaviors _____

d. Desires _____

e. Priorities _____

What difference does the Holy Spirit make in your life? What difference should He make? Some people act as if the Holy Spirit is a tow truck—there to help them out if they get in trouble. But that's not the picture we see in Scripture.

Read 1 John 3:6. What is one effect of the Holy Spirit in the life of a believer?

_____

_____

_____

The passage above doesn't teach that we will ever be to the point where we no longer sin. It does mean that our lives will not be characterized by habitual sin. That's one piece of evidence that God's Spirit is at work in you—the decreasing desire to habitually sin.

REACT

Satan wants to rob you of your confidence in Christ and the assurance of your salvation. This lesson has shown you that you can count on God to do what He promised, and you can count on God to hold on to you.

What reasons do you have to doubt God?

_____

_____

_____

What should you do when doubts come? Remember God's promises. Go back and commit to memory some of the Scriptures in this lesson, especially John 10:28 and Romans 8:38–39. Read and reflect on 2 Peter 1:4 and Peter's confession that God has given us "great and precious promises." Defeat Satan's attacks using the same weapon Jesus used—the knowledge of God's Word.

Based on the Scriptures in this lesson, are your doubts justified? Why or why not?

_____

_____

_____

_____

Salvation is a free gift that God offers to you. Jesus Christ paid the price so that you and I can live forever in heaven with God. There is nothing I can do to make my salvation more secure and nothing I can do to lose it.

Sin does, however, have consequences. Like a wound, sin can leave a scar. Sin affects you and those around you. Forgiveness is certain, but the effects of sin often are long-lasting. Therefore, it is important to not take forgiveness and salvation for granted. Even though our sins are forgiven, we can't live with a disregard for sin's consequences.

Don't let anything—or anyone—ever rob you of your confidence in Christ. Remember: Your salvation depends on what He has done for you, not on what you do for Him. Your salvation is a free gift and a firm foundation—that can never be shaken.

BILLY GRAHAM
The Journey

What are three truths you learned in this study, and how will you apply each truth to your daily life?

1. _____

_____

_____

_____

2. _____

_____

_____

_____

_____

3. _____

_____

_____

_____

3

The
Unending
Battle

T O GET THE MOST FROM THIS STUDY GUIDE, READ
pages 94–103 of *The Journey.*

---

*The Christian life isn't a playground but a battlefield.
None of us is exempt from problems and troubles.*

BILLY GRAHAM
The Journey

THINK ABOUT IT

*We are always in the forge or on the anvil; by trials God is
shaping us for higher things.*

—HENRY WARD BEECHER[1]

*Dear friends, do not be surprised at the painful trial you
are suffering, as though something strange were happening
to you.*

—1 PETER 4:12

It is no secret that life is a battle. Our best-laid plans often are derailed by unexpected events, problems, and things we just don't understand. Even when we are trying to do something positive that will make a lasting impression for God, we find ourselves struggling. Why? Has God confused us so that He can watch us scramble? Not at all! God has no joy in seeing His people struggle, yet we all do it. Our struggles can be the result of our being off track, or they can be designed to get us back on track.

Problems and troubles are universal—we all face them! The difference is that God sees His children through their problems; those who don't know Him are left to figure out things for themselves.

REWIND

Describe a time when your plans were redirected by an unexpected problem or situation.

_____

_____

_____

_____

What was the tone of your prayer regarding this situation?

_____ I didn't pray.

_____ I was angry.

_____ I was frustrated.

_____ I had a martyr syndrome.

_____ I was thankful.

_____ Other: _____

Some Christians believe that their faith is a guarantee that there will be no more problems. However, those of us who have been Christians for a while know that isn't true. Throughout Scripture we see examples of men and women who faced serious problems and remained strong in their faith. What was the difference? Were they better people than us? No, they were just like us. The main difference probably is how people view problems. Some view them as obstacles that can't be overcome; others see them as opportunities for God to do something spectacular.

Think about the last major problem you had. Which statement below best describes the outcome of that situation?

_____ I was stopped in my tracks and forced to develop a new strategy.

_____ I was given the opportunity to see God at work in an unexpected way.

_____ I tried to get through it to the best of my ability.

JOURNEY THROUGH GOD'S WORD

Have you ever declared something to be a miracle? What qualifies something as miraculous? Do we still see miracles today? These are great questions because we use the word *miracle* to describe everything from a last-minute victory by our favorite team to passing tests we thought we would fail. This is another one of those terms that we use a lot but don't really understand.

In the Bible, miracles always are tied to God's activity, and they happen for the purpose of showing people His character and purposes. Miracles happen in nature, in history, and in the lives of everyday people.

In the Old Testament, the words *sign* and *wonder* are used to indicate a miracle. There are many situations in which *signs and wonders* appear in tandem. A sign was an object, a daily activity, or an unexpected action of God. *Signs* point people to God. *Wonders* are special manifestations of God's power.

In the New Testament, *sign* carries the same basic meaning as in the Old Testament. However, signs also indicated divine authority. The Gospel of John includes many references to signs that pointed out Jesus' divine nature. *Wonders,* on the other hand, were situations that would cause the observer to be amazed. These most often referred to God's work.[2]

The truth is that the very act of salvation is a miracle. God's concern for His people is a miracle. God's provision for us also is miraculous. Everyday events qualify as signs and wonders. We must be careful not to overlook God's involvement in our daily lives.

There are people today who constantly look for signs and wonders—miracles—as evidence of God's work in their lives. But if we base our faith on a continual display of miraculous events, we will become spiritually frustrated. God doesn't have to prove to us who He is. Our faith cannot become dependent on God's providing a bigger, better miracle each day. We should trust God because of who He is, not what He does to prove it.

RETHINK

What is your greatest desire in life?

_____ Popularity

_____ Wealth

_____ Peace

_____ Possessions

_____ Security

_____ Other: _____

Read John 14:27. Which of the above did Jesus see as important enough to leave with us?

_____

_____

_____

People chase after many things in life, believing that one of them will bring real peace. But lasting peace cannot be found apart from an intimate relationship with God. When we are in a growing relationship with God, we will find peace in three ways:

1. *Peace with God* (Romans 5:1).

   Before you accepted Jesus Christ as your Lord and Savior, you were God's enemy. That changed, however, when you became a child of God. You no longer are subject to eternity in hell. You are at peace with the Creator of the universe.

2. *Peace in our hearts.*

   Once the threat of eternal punishment is removed, we can live with a sense of gratitude rather than dread. The peace that you have inside is the direct result of God's Spirit living inside you. As He moves in and takes over, you gain the third kind of peace.

3. *Peace with others.*

   When we see other people from God's perspective, we cannot be in conflict with them. We will embrace the ministry of reconciliation and work to lead others first to faith in God, and then to grow in that faith.

What does your level of peace say about your relationship with God?

_____ I'm in a perfect relationship with God.

_____ I've got some room to grow.

_____ I need my batteries recharged.

_____ I need some peace in my life.

What have you tried in search of peace?

_____

_____

_____

Since God is the source of perfect peace, what do you think you should do in order to achieve peace in your life?

_____

_____

_____

REFLECT

Spiritual conflict is real. Some people call it spiritual warfare. Pick the term that suits you, but realize that we are in a battle. On one side, we have God and the victory He brings into our lives. On the other side, we have Satan and his attempts to confuse, confound, and frustrate us. It's a tug-of-war with us being the ropes.

This is a serious battle—not something to be taken lightly. Our effectiveness as God's children hangs in the balance. Satan wants to render you useless for God's purposes. God wants to accomplish great things through your life. If we don't take this battle seriously, we might fall victim to one or more of the following mistakes in our thinking.

1. **Evil isn't real.**

   Some people argue that there is no such thing as evil. They can easily believe that anything goes. This line of thinking, though inconsistent with the Christian life, is more common than you might think.

How do you know evil is real?

_____

_____

_____

What determines right and wrong for you?

_____ I do what seems right at the time.

_____ I do what brings me happiness.

_____ I do what God says is right.

_____ There is no standard of right and wrong.

2. **Evil is real, but we'll never be able to overcome it.**
   Because evil is so prevalent, some people see the
   battle as one that can't be won. Therefore, they
   simply give in and give up. They might see God and
   Satan as equal powers in a battle in which the advantage swings from side to side.

**Read Colossians 2:15. What does this verse say about the
battle between God and Satan?**

_____

_____

_____

_____

Satan is real and powerful. However, God also is real and all-powerful! That's a small difference in wording, but it is of enormous significance. If you know Jesus Christ, you are on the winning side, no matter what you see happening around you.

3. **Evil is real, but I must fight it on my own.**

    God has given you all the resources you need to fight the battles you face. Yet, you and I often try to wage these battles without drawing on God's strength. Fighting this battle without God will wear you down and leave you susceptible to Satan's attacks. Our strength for the battle is our relationship with Jesus Christ.

How do we gain victory each day in the midst of this spiritual conflict? The answer, I'm convinced, can be stated very simply: The key to spiritual victory is to stay close to God. Remember: The closer you are to God, the farther you are from the devil.

BILLY GRAHAM
The Journey

Based on your relationship with Jesus Christ, how prepared are you for battle?

_____ Highly prepared and equipped

_____ Prepared but vulnerable in certain ways

_____ I know where to get my shield if I need it.

_____ I am not ready for battle.

What can you do to be better prepared to fight this battle?

_____

_____

_____

_____

_____

_____

Read Zephaniah 3:17. What is the meaning of this verse in your life?

_____

_____

_____

How can you stay strong for the battle? The answer was written many years ago by a man named James.

Read James 4:7–8. What is James's prescription for spiritual success?

S _____

R _____

C _____

To submit to God means to turn over to God every area of life. That's easy to say, but hard to do! Every concern of life must be laid at Jesus' feet. Resisting the devil requires constant readiness on our part. When he is resisted, Satan is defeated. Drawing close to God puts distance between you and Satan. You can't be close to God and close to Satan at the same time because Satan can't be where God is.

Read Psalm 144:2. Rewrite this verse in your own words reflecting your dependence on God.

_____

_____

_____

_____

REACT

How and when do you come near to God? Is He a parachute to land you safely when needed? Is He a physician to heal you when you are broken? Or is He a constant companion throughout life's journey? Coming near to God requires you to continually remember two truths.

If you know Jesus Christ, you have a personal relationship with God. God is your companion, not a distant ogre denying you passage across a bridge. This is a real comfort to us when we face the battles of life.

Read Hebrews 10:22. What reason do you have not to draw near to Him?

_____

_____

_____

Because you know Jesus Christ, you have a personal relation-ship with fellow believers. You are not in this thing alone! No matter what you are facing, there is someone like you who has gone through something similar. We can draw strength from each other as we grow closer together.

Which of the following activities are part of your normal routine?

_____ Praying with other believers

_____ Worshiping with other believers

_____ Studying God's Word together

_____ Sharing concerns with other believers

_____ Encouraging other believers

_____ Fellowshipping with other believers

What can you do on a daily basis to stay close to God? You must spend time with Him—daily. Too many believers rely on a once-per-week experience to strengthen their spiritual lives. So, how do you develop a daily time with God?

1. *Set aside a time.*
   If your relationship with God is important, you'll set aside time to work on it. You manage to find time for other things that are important, don't you? Give God your best minutes of the day, not the leftovers.

What is your response?

_____ **I commit to spending 10 minutes alone with God**

every day at _____**.**

_____ **I will not give any of my time to God.**

2. *Develop a pattern.*
   Consider including Bible reading, prayer, and reflection in your time with God. When reading the Bible, have a plan that will move you through the entire Bible in a reasonable amount of time. When you pray, don't simply give God a "to do" list; express your concerns and joys. Ask Him to keep you in the center of His will.

3. *Practice God's presence all day long.*

   Pray for those people you encounter. As you drive, whisper a prayer for the people you see along the road. God is with you every moment of every day. Develop the habit of communicating with Him regularly.

What are the instructions in each of the following passages?

1 Thessalonians 5:17

_____

_____

_____

Psalm 119:97

_____

_____

_____

Psalm 145:18

_____

_____

_____

_____

_____

We are not helpless in this life; God has promised His Spirit to those who trust Him with their lives and commit to living for Him. How you face life is your daily choice—face life with God by your side or face life alone.

> *Learn to practice God's presence every waking hour.*
> *Discipline yourself to stay close to God. He alone is your*
> *security.*
>
> BILLY GRAHAM
> *The Journey*

What are three truths you learned in this study, and how will you apply each truth to your daily life?

1. _____

_____

_____

2. _____

_____

_____

3. _____

_____

_____

4

Our
Constant
Helper

T O GET THE MOST FROM THIS STUDY GUIDE, READ
pages 134–142 of *The Journey*.

> *What makes Christians different from everyone else is*
> *that God Himself lives within them by His Holy Spirit.*
> *When we come to Christ and give our lives to Him,*
> *God actually takes up residence within us.*
>
> BILLY GRAHAM
> *The Journey*

THINK ABOUT IT

God commands us to be filled with the Spirit; and if we
aren't filled, it's because we're living beneath our privileges.
— DWIGHT L. MOODY[1]

But you will receive power when the Holy Spirit comes
on you.

—ACTS 1:8

When you enter into a faith relationship with God, His Spirit moves into your life and, if allowed, lives through you. For some people, this is a comforting fact because they know that God has their best interest in mind. For others, this is cause for concern because they believe that they will never again get to do anything they want to do. They are more than willing to accept the eternal benefits of salvation, but they have a tough time with God's involvement in their daily lives.

If you've ever performed any kind of mechanical task, you might have been forced to improvise on your tool selection. For instance, you might have used a kitchen knife in place of a screwdriver or pliers instead of the appropriate wrench.

Each of us is a tool in God's hands, and through the Holy Spirit, God works to use us in the best way possible. We can choose to be something God never intended, but then we become the kitchen knife doubling as a screwdriver—not the best tool for the job.

REWIND

If the Holy Spirit had free reign in your life, what would change?

_____

_____

_____

What keeps you from giving God full control of your life?

_____

_____

_____

_____

As believers, we are different because God, by way of the Holy Spirit, lives inside us. This means that God occupies each person with whom He has a faith relationship. We can't hide from Him or leave Him home while we do something else. He is with us every moment of our lives.

Read John 14:16–17. What is the condition upon which this promise is made?

_____

_____

_____

_____

Read Romans 8:9. If you are in a relationship with Jesus Christ, who lives inside you?

_____

_____

_____

The Holy Spirit's presence in your life is permanent. He doesn't need to be coaxed back into your life. It is because of God's Spirit that you are able to determine right from wrong. The Holy Spirit also draws you to confess your sin. Without the Holy Spirit's encouragement, you would never willingly choose to repent.

JOURNEY THROUGH GOD'S WORD

The Father, the Son, and the Holy Spirit are the ways God reveals Himself to the human race. This relationship is often referred to as the Trinity. The doctrine of the Trinity is distinctively Christian. The term _trinity_ never appears in Scripture (which has caused some skeptics to doubt its validity). The Trinity does not describe three different Gods, nor does it describe God in terms of being the Father only.

In Deuteronomy 6:4, God is described as being one. This was in response to the threat of polytheism that was prominent in the early days of Israel. The full revelation of the Trinity is drawn from the New Testament after the establishment of Jesus' ministry. The Trinity can be summed up in four statements:

1. God is One. God is the same from the Old Testament to the New Testament.

2. God is One, but involves Himself in redemption in three different ways. He is fully God, fully Spirit, and fully the Son of God.

3. The only way to begin to understand the Trinity is to participate in the salvation experience.

4. The doctrine of the Trinity is a mystery[2]—we will never fully understand—but it is still true.

Describing God in terms of the Trinity allows for the reality that God is fully God, Jesus Christ is fully God, and the Holy Spirit is fully God. There is no other way to explain Jesus' divinity.

Knowing that the Holy Spirit lives inside you is step one; submitting to His power in your life is the second step. Let's take a closer look at our need to submit to God's power in our lives.

RETHINK

What are your two greatest needs in life?

_____ Forgiveness

_____ Goodness

_____ Wealth

_____ Fame

_____ Appearance

_____ Other: _____

There are two basic spiritual needs in everyone's life—forgiveness and goodness. Both require intervention from the outside; we can't do these alone. But how do we develop these strengths in our lives? Forgiveness and goodness work from the inside out. Most attempts at self-improvement fail.

> *If we are to live the way God meant us to live . . . if we*
> *are to become more like Christ . . . if we are to travel*
> *our journey wisely . . . then we need both God's for-*
> *giveness and goodness. We need to work of the Son for*
> *us, and we need the work of the Holy Spirit in us. To*
> *the great gift of forgiveness God adds the great gift of*
> *the Holy Spirit.*
>
> BILLY GRAHAM
> *The Journey*

Read Romans 7:18–19. Can you relate to Paul's words? Why or why not?

_____

_____

_____

_____

Many people struggle because they attempt to do things on their own. However, the Bible teaches that we should rely on the strength of the Holy Spirit. Anything God asks us to do, He empowers us to do. God's empowerment in the life of a believer is through the Holy Spirit. On life's journey, the Holy Spirit is our constant companion.

Reflect on a time when you have relied on your own power rather than the power of the Holy Spirit. What was the outcome of that situation?

_____

_____

_____

How might it have turned out if you had relied on the Holy Spirit?

_____

_____

_____

REFLECT

Who is the Holy Spirit? Oddly, some people get their ideas about the Holy Spirit from somewhere other than the Bible. In an attempt to personalize the Holy Spirit, many people develop ideas about Him that are far from the truth.

Which of the following is true?

The Holy Spirit is . . .

_____ An impersonal spiritual force moving about the earth

_____ A feeling or an emotion

_____ A gift-giver

_____ The abiding presence of God

_____ Other: _____

There are three things the Bible tells us about the Holy Spirit. Let's take a look at each one.

1. **The Holy Spirit is a person.**
   The Holy Spirit isn't an "it" but a "He." The Holy Spirit has all of God's attributes because He is fully God. He speaks to us, instructs us, intercedes for us, hears us, guides us, and so forth. Even though He knows the truth, we can lie to Him and disappoint Him.

Read Romans 8:16. What does this verse say about the Holy Spirit?

_____

_____

_____

_____

2.   The Holy Spirit is a power.
     God works through the Holy Spirit to accomplish
     His will.

Read the following passages and write briefly what each one says about the Holy Spirit's power.

Genesis 1:2

_____

_____

_____

Job 33:4

_____

_____

_____

Judges 15:14

_____

_____

_____

Exodus 31:3

_____

_____

_____

The Holy Spirit also has the power to convict you of sin and lead you to a faith relationship with God. It is God's Spirit that draws people to Him. It is God's Spirit that intercedes on our behalf.

Match each verse with its message. [Answers can be found at the end of the chapter.]

a. God's Word will accomplish its purpose.

b. The Spirit produces spiritual change.

c. The Spirit guarantees the future.

_____ 2 Corinthians 1:22   _____ John 3:6

_____ Isaiah 55:11

3. **The Holy Spirit is God.**
   God is divine; Jesus is divine; the Holy Spirit is divine.

What does 2 Corinthians 3:17 say about God?

_____

_____

_____

Apart from God's involvement in our lives, we could never pursue godliness. But because the Holy Spirit is at work in our lives, we can become more like God in the way that we deal with other people. Because of God's Spirit, we are concerned about the spiritual conditions of those we know. This is all because the Holy Spirit delivers God's nature to us; otherwise, we would be consumed with ourselves.

We can agree that the Holy Spirit has come, but why did He come? The Holy Spirit has been involved in everything from the creation of the world to the birth of Jesus Christ. However, the Holy Spirit was released to the disciples of Jesus at Pentecost (see Acts 2). Whereas Jesus had been physically present with the disciples before His death, He promised to continue to be with them after His death. That is why He sent the Holy Spirit. So, what does the Holy Spirit do?

Read the following Scriptures and list the work of the Holy Spirit described in each.

John 16:8

_____

_____

_____

John 16:13

_____

_____

_____

_____

Acts 1:8

_____

_____

_____

_____

As you can see, the Holy Spirit came so that we can fulfill the purposes for which God designed us. You have a specific task through which you will find your greatest fulfillment and joy. This task might be related to your vocation, hobbies, social life, family life, or any other aspect of life. It might involve one or more of these areas.

Are you fulfilled in your spiritual life?

_____ Yes

_____ No

_____ Sometimes

Explain the reasons for your response.

_____

_____

_____

REACT

You have a constant Helper who is ready to take you on the journey of your life. God has plans that you can't imagine, and He intends to use you in ways that you never dreamed possible. Your purpose in life isn't a mystery; it is spelled out in Scripture. You've already read the Scripture and discovered God's desire for you, so let's see just how willing you are to do what it is He asks you to do.

Are you allowing God to convict you of sin? This is different from identifying sin in your life or the lives of people you know. It's one thing to recognize sin; it's another thing to be convicted.

What does it mean to be convicted of sin?

_____

_____

_____

_____

To be convicted means to be found guilty against the standard. We have two choices when it comes to sin—stand convicted or adjust the standard. Which one are you more likely to do?

Are you allowing the Holy Spirit to teach and guide you? Some people come to the Bible with an idea and then look for Scriptures to back it up. That's not learning and being guided! Truth originates in God and flows from Him though His Word, His Spirit, and His people.

What are three spiritual truths you have learned in the past seven days?

1. _____

_____

2. _____

_____

3. _____

_____

In what setting did you learn these truths?

_____

_____

_____

Why would people not want to know God's truth? Probably because they don't want to make the changes it demands.

Is this true of you?

_____

Are you telling others about Christ? The work of spreading the word about God isn't reserved for professional ministers and church leaders. It is the work of everyone who knows Jesus Christ as Lord and Savior. If you review Acts 1:8, the text doesn't suggest that some people *might* choose to be witnesses. It says, "You will be my witnesses."

When was the last time you shared your faith with someone?

_____

_____

_____

List three people with whom you should share your faith now.

_____

_____

_____

There is one final reason God sent His Holy Spirit—so that you and I can become more like Christ. We can't become like Him on our own; we need help. That is why God sent us His Constant Helper.

If you try to live your life without the help of the Holy Spirit, you will be disappointed. You must turn to Him daily and ask Him to lead you where He wants you to go. Why not do that right now?

Jesus said, the Spirit will help us tell others about Christ. The Spirit goes ahead of us when we witness—preparing the way, giving us the words, and granting us courage. The Spirit truly helps us witness.

BILLY GRAHAM
The Journey

What are three truths you learned in this study, and how will you apply each truth to your daily life?

1. _____

   _____

   _____

   _____

2. _____

_____

_____

_____

3. _____

_____

_____

_____

Answers to Scripture matching on page 74 —

a. Isaiah 55:11; b. John 3:6; c. 2 Corinthians 1:22

5

Strength
for
Each Day

T O GET THE MOST FROM THIS STUDY GUIDE, READ
pages 143–152 of *The Journey.*

*Becoming a Christian is the work of a moment; being
a Christian is the work of a lifetime.*

BILLY GRAHAM
The Journey

THINK ABOUT IT

*I've never been one who thought the good Lord should make
life easy; I've just asked Him to make me strong.*

—EVA BOWRING[1]

*But grow in the grace and knowledge of our Lord and
Savior Jesus Christ.*

—2 PETER 3:18

We never know what challenges are ahead of us. Life can be going just fine and then something happens to disrupt a moment, a day, or sometimes a lifetime. The true test of Christianity isn't how one responds to the good days; the true test is how one responds when life gets tough.

If we are going to stand up under the pressures of life, we must begin to see the true source of our strength. Even Christians can make the mistake of relying on themselves first and turning to God as a last resort. However, it shouldn't be that way. God, through His Spirit, gives us the strength we need for the trials we face each day. He promises to sustain us if we will only rely upon Him.

REWIND

What are some situations you have encountered in which you turned to God after having exhausted all of your other options?

_____

_____

_____

_____

How might things have been different if you had turned to God first?

_____

_____

_____

The situations we encounter are opportunities for us to mature our faith. Conversion is the beginning of the spiritual journey, but there's more. We make a mistake to secure our places in heaven and never grow.

Read Luke 8:1–15. What type of soil are you?

_____ Wayside soil being raided by Satan

_____ Rocky soil lacking room for roots to grow

_____ Thorny soil choking out new growth with the cares of the world

_____ Fertile soil producing fruit that reveals God's character

If you aren't fertile soil, what is keeping you from growing in your faith?

_____

_____

_____

It only takes a moment to become a Christian, but being a Christian is a lifelong experience.

JOURNEY THROUGH GOD'S WORD

Have you ever heard someone say, "I'm going through tribulation right now"? _Tribulation_ is another term that is used primarily among believers for the purpose of describing some trouble they are experiencing. Though tribulation and problems seem synonymous, tribulation has a unique meaning according to Scripture.

We generally call any unpleasant situation _tribulation._ The New Testament teaches us to expect tribulation

---

because of our faith. The concept reaches back into the Old Testament for its original meaning.

The Hebrew word for *tribulation* means "narrow" or "compressed." It also can mean "affliction." The Greek term carries much the same meaning—severe constriction, narrowing, or pressing together. There are a few things we should remember about tribulation.

1. Our tribulations will be patterned after the suffering of Christ (1 Peter 4:1).

2. Our tribulation is the way in which we participate in Christ's suffering (2 Corinthians 1:5).

3. Our tribulations mold us into the likeness of Christ (Romans 5:3).

4. Our tribulations teach us to encourage each other (2 Corinthians 1:4).

People who suggest that the Christian life will be void of problems really don't understand Scripture. The Bible teaches that the absence of trouble is more unusual than its presence in the lives of those who know God.[2]

How do you view the trouble you face? Do you see it as a learning and growing opportunity, or does it render you powerless? When you see tribulation as something that makes you more like God, you can embrace its value even while going through tough times. That is one of the true marks of authentic, maturing faith in God.

Do you have strength for each day? Is life overwhelming you? There are two facts that should bring you comfort. First, all believers go through tough times. Second, our tough times mature us so that we can be an encouragement for people we meet. It might not be a pleasant situation, but it certainly is a valuable situation.

RETHINK

What is your goal for your life?

_____

_____

_____

_____

What is God's goal for your life?

_____

_____

_____

Explain any differences between the responses above.

_____

_____

_____

God's goal for your life is for you to become more like Christ. You become more like Christ through discipleship—the intentional effort to learn more and more about God.

Read the following Scriptures:

2 Corinthians 3:18

Galatians 4:19

1 John 3:2

Plot your progress on the line below by placing an X where you started and a Y where you are right now.

Without God in my life   Just like God

_____

What is the instruction in Philippians 2:15?

_____

_____

_____

It is the responsibility of every believer to become more like Christ and less like the world. In order to do that, we must replace all ungodly influences with godly influences.

Think about your leisure time. What are you most likely to do when you have extra time?

_____ Watch television

_____ Read a magazine

_____ Exercise

_____ Go to a movie

_____ Listen to music

_____ Study the Bible

_____ Relax

_____ Work on a hobby

_____ Shop

_____ Talk on the phone

_____ Other: _____

What is the spiritual value of the activity you checked?

_____

_____

_____

What are you doing to become like Christ? Are you more concerned about other things? If so, it should come as no surprise
that you are not growing in your faith.

REFLECT

What does it mean to be like Christ? It means Christ becomes Lord of every area of our lives. Why are some Christians so negative and critical? Why are some so sour or grumpy or arrogant or impatient? Why are some so anxious and filled with worry, or lazy and undisciplined, or undependable and irresponsible? Why are some so domineering or harsh toward others? God calls us to be like Christ.

BILLY GRAHAM
The Journey

When Christ takes over control of our lives, we will see His effect in three areas: our character, our actions, and our attitudes. The Holy Spirit can work in our lives to produce God's character if we will set aside our own character and let Him work. Each of us has God's character residing in us. If His character isn't showing, it's because our personal character is blocking the path.

Reflect on your last conflict. When the situation was over, had the other person encountered you or God? Which character was in control of your life?

Because we have God's Spirit, we have the capacity to act in ways that are consistent with His nature. What you are on the inside is revealed in your behavior. When you encounter a problem, your actions will tell the world who is really in charge of your life.

Think about the last time you placed an order at a restaurant and you experienced a problem. What did your response say about your relationship with God?

Finally, once God's Spirit has control of your character and actions, your attitudes will conform to His attitudes. You will begin to value people the same way God values people. There will be no prejudice or rush to judgment. Instead, you will love people because you know that God cannot hate anyone; He can hate what someone does, but He doesn't hate the person.

Why is it so difficult for us to accept people without accepting their values and/or behavior? What categories of people are on your "most difficult to love" list?

_____

_____

_____

So, how do we make this radical change? It can only happen as we give control of our lives to the Holy Spirit. We can't change ourselves; only God can change us. Here's a recipe to make this happen in your life.

1. **Repent.**

   Ask God to reveal to you areas of your life that you have not given over to His control. If you ask God, He will show you those areas.

Read Psalm 139:23–24. What is there about your life that God doesn't know?

_____

_____

_____

2. **Submit.**

It's one thing to know what to do; it's another thing to actually do it. Satan doesn't want you to yield to God's Spirit. He wants to keep you frustrated and ineffective. When Jesus Christ moves into your life, your old nature isn't displaced.

What is the advice in Luke 9:23?

_____

_____

_____

What is the advice in Colossians 3:5?

_____

_____

_____

_____

What is the declaration in Galatians 2:20?

_____

_____

_____

_____

Submitting to the Holy Spirit means giving Him control of every area of your life. There is a temptation to focus on one area to the exclusion of other areas. Yet there is a commandment regarding how we are to deal with our old life.

Read Ephesians 4:22–24. What is the instruction in these verses?

_____

_____

_____

Remember the words of James 4:7–8. Rewrite this passage as a motto for your life.

_____

_____

_____

3. Obey.

Sometimes we wonder if we are doing what is right. But we can easily eliminate that dilemma by obeying God. God will never command us to do wrong. God will never command us to do something that violates His Word. There are a lot of decisions that could be made easier if we would just pay attention to what God said in His Word.

Read Psalm 119:101. What is the purpose of God's Word?

_____

_____

_____

What aspects of life are not addressed specifically or in principle in God's Word?

_____

_____

_____

In addition to obeying God's Word, we must obey His Spirit. We can't obey God's Spirit if we aren't paying attention to His Spirit. God's Spirit will not contradict His Word because God cannot contradict Himself.

REACT

Repentance, submission, and obedience must become the norm for our daily lives. Only as we practice these disciplines can we see God's Spirit work more naturally through our lives. Spirituality isn't something that we put on once each week and wear to church; it is the essence of who we are as children of God.

Think about your daily schedule and consider some adjustments you can make to free up time to spend with God. Becoming like Christ will produce Christlike humility in your life. As you develop humility, you will be more and more willing to lay your life before God every day of your life.

Read Galatians 5:22–23. Rank yourself from 1 to 5 with 5 being the maximum in each of the following characteristics:

_____ Love

_____ Joy

_____ Peace

_____ Patience

_____ Kindness

_____ Goodness

_____ Faithfulness

_____ Gentleness

_____ Self-control

If you aren't making time with God a priority, growing in your faith will be difficult. Rather than seeing these characteristics in your life, you will see their opposites. This is the root of hypocrisy—claiming to believe one thing but acting in ways that are inconsistent with those beliefs. This is what causes so many nonbelievers to reject calls to faith in Christ.

What can you do to keep from being an obstacle to someone who is not a believer in Jesus Christ?

_____

_____

_____

God worked a miracle in the life of Paul. He transformed him from a man who lived to persecute and kill Christians into one of the most effective evangelists the world has ever known. Rather than seek out people to kill, Paul sought out people to save. But it wasn't Paul's effort that led to that change. Only God through the Holy Spirit could accomplish that miracle in Paul's life.

God wants to accomplish the same miracle in your life. He wants to transform you into a spiritual force that He can use to accomplish His purposes.

What keeps you from yielding to God's control in your life?

_____

_____

_____

What might change if God gets total control of your life?

_____

_____

_____

How many problems would we avoid if we knew God's Word and obeyed it? The Bible doesn't give us a rule for every conceivable situation, but it does cover far more than most of us realize. It also gives us principles by which we are to guide our lives. God's Word isn't to be debated or dissected; it is to be done.

BILLY GRAHAM
The Journey

What are three truths you learned in this study, and how will you apply each truth to your daily life?

1. _____

_____

_____

_____

2. _____

_____

_____

_____

3. _____

_____

_____

_____

6

Suffering
and
Loss

To GET THE MOST FROM THIS STUDY GUIDE, READ pages 215–224 of *The Journey*.

Nothing demonstrates human frailty more forcefully than pain. It reminds us life is fragile and ultimately outside our control. Suffering and pain come to us all, and the real question is this: How should we react?

BILLY GRAHAM
The Journey

THINK ABOUT IT

Although the world is full of suffering, it is also full of the overcoming of it.

—HELEN KELLER[1]

Though he brings grief, he will show compassion, so great is his unfailing love.

—LAMENTATIONS 3:32

Emotional pain can come when we least expect it, and it reminds us of the fact that there is a God and He is in charge. Pain also reminds us that we are on a nonstop train toward the day when we will no longer exist on this earth.

Sometimes pain causes us to question God. We wonder why we must go through certain situations. We wonder if God is trying to get our attention or teach us a lesson. Some people just can't handle life's sufferings and loss.

What happens when you experience pain and suffering? Do you turn inward? Outward? Upward? Do you look for the lesson or the loophole? Do you praise God or sing a gloomy song? The fact is that your response to suffering and loss reveals your real identity in Christ.

REWIND

When was the last time you suffered a significant pain or loss?

_____

_____

_____

_____

How did you respond to that situation?

_____

_____

_____

Life is unpredictable and full of unexpected events. Many people, in order to brace themselves for the unexpected events in life, seek consolation in their horoscopes or through psychics, yet the Bible tells us how hopeless (and even dangerous) these things really are.

Read James 4:14. What does God say to those who claim to know what tomorrow will bring?

_____

_____

_____

Because we know that pain and suffering are real, we try to insulate ourselves against their effects. Yet we are never prepared enough for the situations we encounter. We think we can count on people, employers, finances, appearance, and intelligence. Yet we know that people let us down, employers lay us off, finances are swallowed up in unexpected bills, appearance is fleeting, and intelligence is subject to a myriad of limitations. We really can't count on these things.

What can you count on 100 percent of the time?

_____

_____

_____

Was God on your list? Why or why not?

_____

_____

_____

JOURNEY THROUGH GOD'S WORD

Human suffering is a normal part of life. The Bible teaches that suffering is inevitable. It also warns us that Christians

---

sometimes suffer more than people who do not know Jesus Christ as Savior.

There are three sources of suffering: physical problems or limitations, natural disasters, and human actions. Physical causes can be subdivided into diseases, physical and psychological limitations, and mental illness. Natural causes include storms, fire, floods, and earthquakes. Human actions encompass harming oneself or others.

Some people question God's reasoning for allowing pain and suffering. The short answer is that man is unable to comprehend God's ways. God allows suffering for reasons that ultimately reveal His character.

Psalm 7:12–16 teaches that sin causes suffering. But all suffering is not the result of sin. Some people make the mistake of trying to trace every instance of suffering and pain to some specific personal action.

In spite of the fact that suffering and pain are part of life, God remains in control (2 Samuel 14:14). Some suffering is used by God to teach His people. Suffering reminds us that we are God's creation, totally dependent on Him for our very existence. Because God loves us, He will use whatever means necessary to guide us in His ways.

Suffering is not a reason for defeat. James 1:2–12 teaches that suffering should be cause for rejoicing because it produces maturity and godly character in us.[2]

The one thing we can count on in this life is God. God is always interested in the well-being of His children. Because He cares for us, He often uses life's everyday pains to teach us and mature us. It is hard to be thankful for the pain, but we always can be thankful for the lessons we learn through the pain.

RETHINK

What is the appropriate response to pain and suffering?

_____

_____

_____

How should we react to pain and suffering? Scripture teaches two important truths:

1. *Be on guard against pain's dangers.*
   The natural response to any pain is to turn inward and begin analyzing the problem. In doing so, we shut out others and obsess about things that might not be as big a problem as we perceive them to be.

When you are in pain, what do you do? (Check all that apply.)

_____ Lash out at loved ones

_____ Have self-pity

_____ Get mad at God

_____ Focus only on my pain

_____ Other: _____

Read Psalm 31:10. When have you felt the same as the psalmist?

_____

_____

_____

One of the most effective ways to deal with pain is to pray for others, not just yourself. Sometimes your physical limitations uniquely equip you to focus your prayers on the needs of other people.

2. *Ask God to help you learn the lessons that the pain can teach.*
   God can—and will—use your pain for your benefit.

What is something that was painful that has produced long-lasting, positive results in your life?

_____

_____

_____

Pain teaches that life is fragile; therefore we should be thankful for every breath we have. Too many times we focus on what's wrong rather than what's right. Take a few moments and thank God for the life you have.

Pain also draws us closer to God. It's easy to forget about God when our lives are good. Pain reminds us of our dependence on God and our need for Him in every aspect of our lives.

> *Above all, when suffering comes, rejoice in the hope we have of heaven because of Christ. No matter what you are going through, someday it will end and you will be with Christ forever. Earth's troubles fade in the light of heaven's hope.*
>
> BILLY GRAHAM
> *The Journey*

Read Psalm 145:18. Based on the truths in this verse, is God near to you? Why or why not?

_____

_____

_____

Suffering calls us to trust God more and more. We know that Jesus Christ suffered in order to secure a place in heaven for each of us. Without Jesus' suffering, you and I would have no hope of gaining entrance to heaven. He suffered so you and I would not suffer eternally. That's how much God loves us.

Are these Scriptures true of you?

2 Corinthians 12:9

_____ Yes   _____ No

2 Corinthians 4:17

_____ Yes   _____ No

REFLECT

One of the most painful of life's emotions is grief. Painful experiences often involve loss of health, friendship, finances, inner peace, or hope. The loss produces an emotion that is called grief. You can grieve the loss of a job as well as the loss of a loved one.

Some people go through experiences that include tremendous personal loss. Hurricanes, tornadoes, wildfires, floods, and other natural disasters can take everything a person has. In recent years, we've see many examples of such situations.

Some people argue that the death of a believer should not induce grief. That's only partly true. When a believer dies, we can celebrate because we know that he or she will be in heaven immediately after death. The grief is for the relationship that we will miss. Grief is a natural and appropriate emotion.

Jesus experienced grief at the death of Lazarus (John 11:35). Jesus knows what it is to lose someone you love. That is why He is uniquely qualified to comfort us in such times. Isaiah 53:3 tells us that Jesus knew what grief was all about. Yet, as believers, our grief is different.

Read 1 Thessalonians 4:13. What makes our grief different?

_____

_____

_____

_____

Our grief isn't an expression of sadness; it is an expression of our love for someone who has passed from our midst. How should we respond when we experience grief?

1. **Don't be surprised by grief.**
   Traumatic events will have an effect on us no matter how prepared we are. Our grief can produce a variety of emotions that include, but are not limited to, anger, dismay, emotional outbursts, and more.

Read John 11:32. How did grief affect the attitude of the speaker?

_____

_____

_____

_____

2. **Turn your grief over to God.**
   God is fully able to take from us those things that we can't handle—that includes our grief.

Read Psalm 55:22. How many burdens does God want from you?

_____ The ones I can't handle

_____ Some of them

_____ None of them

_____ All of them

Why would anyone not turn his or her grief over to God?

_____

_____

_____

_____

You can only turn your grief over to God when you realize the depth of your weaknesses and the depth of God's love. God wants your grief to disappear in His love.

Read 2 Corinthians 1:3–4. What is the message of this passage?

_____

_____

_____

3. **Surround your grief with gratitude.**
   Maybe you can't thank God for the grief, but you can be thankful you have a God to sustain you through the grief. Recount the good times you shared with a loved one. Be thankful that your loved one is now experiencing the joys of heaven—a place you will get to experience one day.

Read Ephesians 5:20. The command of this verse is to give thanks to God in the name of Jesus Christ.

4. **Reach out to someone who also is hurting.**
   Almost everyone is experiencing some sort of pain. One of the best ways to deal with your own pain is to invest in the lives of other people. Grief turns us inward, but compassion turns us outward.

Read Galatians 6:2. Whose burdens should you be carrying?

_____

_____

_____

When you are grieving, ask God to lead you to someone who needs your friendship. Pray for them, spend time with them, listen to them, encourage them, and share God's love with them. In doing so, it will also be therapeutic for you.

REACT

Sometimes life's burdens are so heavy that you don't feel as if you can help anyone else. But sharing the burden lightens the load. We will never understand why God allows disappointment and suffering.

Read 1 Corinthians 13:12. What was Paul's attitude toward understanding life's events?

_____

_____

_____

What can you do? How can you stand up under life's problems? It's a familiar response—stay close to God. You don't have to stand up alone under the pressure because God will provide the strength you need.

We can keep from focusing on ourselves by staying focused on God. If we aren't deliberate in this action, we will default to self-absorption. Then, when the problems persist, we become bitter and we fail to live up to God's purposes for our lives.

Though pain is stressful, it is powerless against your relationship with God. In other words, pain cannot separate you from God.

Read Romans 8:38–39. Think about your life. Has there ever been a time when you've allowed a situation you were facing to separate you from God? Explain.

_____

_____

_____

God isn't going anywhere. If anyone moves, it is you and I. We abandon God's purposes and allow our focus to be on things other than our relationships with God. We separate ourselves from God. We might blame the separation on the suffering or pain, but in reality, the separation is our fault.

> *God's will is for us to become more like Christ, and hardship and suffering are part of this process. . . . For the Christian, faith is real—because it's focused not on ourselves or on our circumstances, but on Christ. In the midst of life's trials and sorrows, is He the focus of your faith?*
> BILLY GRAHAM
> *The Journey*

What are three truths you learned in this study, and how will you apply each truth to your daily life?

1. _____

_____

_____

_____

2. _____

_____

_____

_____

3. _____

_____

_____

_____

NOTES

CHAPTER 1

1. Bob Kelly, *Worth Repeating*, 2003. Grand Rapids, MI: Kregel Publications, 146.

2. *Holman Illustrated Bible Dictionary*, 2003. Nashville, TN: B&H, 160.

CHAPTER 2

1. Bob Kelly, *Worth Repeating*, 321.

2. *Holman Illustrated Bible Dictionary*, 1331–1333.

CHAPTER 3

1. Bob Kelly, *Worth Repeating*, 347.

2. *Holman Illustrated Bible Dictionary*, 1135–1136.

CHAPTER 4

1. Bob Kelly, *Worth Repeating*, 171.

2. *Holman Illustrated Bible Dictionary*, 1625–1627.

CHAPTER 5

1. Bob Kelly, *Worth Repeating*, 322.

2. *Holman Illustrated Bible Dictionary*, 1624–1625.

Chapter 6

1. Bob Kelly, *Worth Repeating*, 326.
2. *Holman Illustrated Bible Dictionary*, 1539.

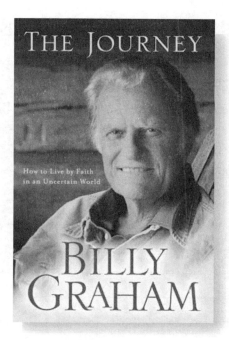

Billy Graham is respected and loved around the world.
The Journey is his magnum opus, the culmination of a
lifetime of experience and ministry. With insight that comes
only from a life spent with God, this book is filled with
wisdom, encouragement, hope, and inspiration for anyone
who wants to live a happier, more fulfilling life.

978-0-8499-1887-2 (PB)

STUDY GUIDE NOTES

STUDY GUIDE NOTES

STUDY GUIDE NOTES

STUDY GUIDE NOTES

STUDY GUIDE NOTES

_____

_____

_____

_____

_____

_____

_____

_____

_____

_____

_____

_____

_____

_____

_____

_____

_____

_____

_____

_____

_____

_____

_____

_____

STUDY GUIDE NOTES

STUDY GUIDE NOTES